VINTAGE VIEWS
of
DEAL & WALMER

Gregory Holyoake

S.B. Publications

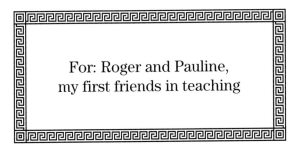

For: Roger and Pauline,
my first friends in teaching

First published in 2010 by S. B. Publications
Tel: 01323 893498
Email: sbpublications@tiscali.co.uk
www.sbpublications.co.uk

ISBN 978-185770-3634

Designed and Typeset by EH Graphics (01273) 515527

VINTAGE VIEWS
of
DEAL & WALMER

'All Aboard the Skylark!'

THE GOLDEN AGE OF DEAL AND WALMER

Deal and Walmer rose in prosperity as Sandwich's fortunes declined. For centuries Deal, as a limb of Sandwich, a principal Cinque Port, was bound by its rules and regulations. This caused animosity between the two towns, particularly when hard-earned dues were payable regularly through ancient laws by the inhabitants of Deal to their wealthy neighbour. Sandwich, as a flourishing medieval port, suffered heavily when its haven began to silt up in Tudor times and the entrance to its harbour, once two miles wide, was rapidly reduced to a mere stream.

Deal provided an alternative to a harbour in the Downs, that vast anchorage between the Kent coast and the Goodwin Sands. A Navy Yard had been established in Stuart times and fleets of Royal Navy warships lay waiting offshore for either supplies, repairs or their instructions from the Admiralty. The Downs provided an important role in providing refuge for sailing ships when it was stormy at sea or when they were becalmed through lack of a suitable wind to carry them further along the English Channel.

Deal and Walmer boatmen enjoyed a lucrative trade in servicing the merchant ships that also swept into the Downs before attempting worldwide voyages. A multitude of services - piloting, salvaging, sweeping for anchors and cables, revictualling and transporting men and letters, supplies and provisions to anchored ships - came under the curious term of 'hovelling'. And, since the towns were conveniently close to France, it would be foolish to deny that boatmen owed much of their accumulated wealth to the nefarious practice of smuggling in this bustling, thriving port.

Deal's new found prosperity brought its freedom. In 1699, William III granted Deal a Charter of Incorporation making it a 'Borough and Market Town', independent of Sandwich.

During the Napoleonic Wars, Deal developed into a garrison town. Vice Admiral Lord Nelson was based at the 'Royal Hotel' when commanded by the Admiralty to make an assault on enemy shipping based at Calais and Boulogne in the summer of 1801. Shortly afterwards Lieutenant-General Sir Arthur Wellesley temporarily resided in a modest dwelling in Castle Road, Walmer, while assembling his troops for an invasion of Portugal in 1808. The town teemed with soldiers and sailors drafted in for these campaigns and boatmen found further profitable employment in ferrying them to their ships before departing for the Continent. Throughout this period of embarkation the town took on an aspect of a holiday.

When hostilities ceased early in the 19th century, military and naval officers with their families returned to this charming seaside town and they built their own grand villas along the foreshore. Aspects of the late Georgian town were recorded in attractive prints and engravings which, although rare and expensive, are avidly sought after by collectors today.

The advent of steamships introduced in the mid-nineteenth century marked a rapid decline in the boatmen's fortunes. Independent of wind power, they left the Port of London and steamed full ahead down the English Channel, without pausing to take on supplies in the Downs. A further blow was dealt by the expansion of the docks at Dover Harbour, a scheme supported by the Duke of Wellington, Lord Warden of the Cinque Ports, when resident at Walmer Castle. Unemployed boatmen faced poverty, starvation and homelessness and, as an alternative to the overcrowded workhouse, contemplated emigration to begin a new life in Australia or New Zealand.

The town received fresh impetus with the opening up of the railways. The line from London via Ramsgate reached Deal in 1847 and from Dover in 1881. Families from London and beyond travelled down to the coast - encouraged by the Bank Holiday Acts of 1871 - for welcome short breaks at the seaside. The splendid South Eastern Hotel was built by one enterprising railway company for its wealthy passengers along the promenade but numerous smaller hotels also benefited from their custom. Deal and Walmer revelled in the holiday trade - shopkeepers doubled their seasonal trade, landladies of boarding houses welcomed paying guests while boatmen organised fishing expeditions or pleasure trips around the Downs.

Summer visitors were attracted by the sea bathing, beach fishing, country walks and boating excursions along the coast. They explored local landmarks - castles, churches, time-ball tower and iron pier while the Royal Marines entertained audiences with regular concerts at the crowded bandstand. Naturally, they wanted souvenirs of their holiday and sent home cheap viewcards to friends and neighbours who had remained at home. Inadvertently, these pictorial views, posted by their thousands in the early years of the twentieth century, record an important era of Deal and Walmer. They encapsulate those last, lingering, Indian summers by the sea prior to the onslaught of the First World War.

Plain postcards were introduced as an experiment by the Austro-Hungarian Empire in 1869. The venture was so successful - sales averaged one million per month - that other countries quickly copied this novelty. The first British postcards printed by the Post Office were placed on sale in the autumn of the following year. One side bore the royal coat of arms, a halfpenny stamp and the legend: 'POSTCARD - THE ADDRESS ONLY TO BE WRITTEN ON THIS SIDE.' The reverse was left blank for a message. Private companies realised the commercial possibilities of producing postcards but their efforts were at first hindered by the tardiness of the Post Office that insisted unofficially printed postcards were liable to the full letter rate: one penny.

Eventually, the Post Office relented to pressure from the public. In 1894, the postage penalty on privately printed postcards was abandoned; by 1902 the message and the address was allowed to be written on the same side as the stamp. The development of photography and printing allowed high quality viewcards to be produced at reasonable prices, particularly in Germany. In Britain, publishers responded to the demand by publishing series of lithographed postcards with pictures of holiday resorts, beauty spots and historic landmarks which visitors bought as souvenirs to send to relatives and friends.

The market was flooded with viewcards. Folk quickly overcame their scruples of scrawling

The Kent Coast Express (Southern Railway) brings holidaymakers to Deal and Walmer.

Passengers board a charabanc opposite the pier to explore the countryside.

messages that might be read by the postman. (Invariably, collectors today turn to the back to decipher the faded message from unknown corresponders.) Postcards were relatively cheap and easily available; they were often sent by people in domestic service, either friends or lovers, who lived only streets away from each other. It was a desperate means of keeping in touch by hard-working servants who could only actually meet in person on their infrequent half days of freedom.

Another regular employment of the postcard was for housekeepers to place an order for their meat or groceries for the day. Requirements could be jotted down first thing in the morning and posted in a convenient pillar box and, since there were numerous collections throughout the day, delivered to the shop by midday and brought round to the back door of the house by delivery boys on their bicycles in plenty of time for cook to prepare the evening meal. It will be noted in Edwardian street scenes ladies are not carrying heavy menial shopping since this would be considered 'quite vulgar'.

Prior to the First World War, the most prolific photographer of topographical views was Lucien Levy. A Frenchman, he also acquired a profitable studio in London in 1905 where he painstakingly developed the thousands of photographs he had taken on his travels across Southern England. Levy confined his subjects to metropolitan landmarks, tourist towns and seaside resorts. His photographic postcards are distinguished by his perfect composition, accurate exposure and lively views, replete with fascinating detail. His street scenes, particularly, are rich in movement and vitality. These highly desirable postcards are instantly recognised by his monogram: 'L.L.'.

One of the most prolific painters of postcards was Walter H Young (1870 - 1920) who worked for a variety of publishers and signed his name with the pseudonym, 'Jotter'. He originated from Sheffield, was articled to a solicitor but decided on a career as an artist. He instantly attained success by opening a large studio in London from whence he travelled the length and breadth of the country, engaged in a variety of commercial projects ranging from designing theatrical and railway posters to painting magazine covers and literally thousands of viewcards.

Around the turn of the century Young was commissioned by Raphael Tuck to paint a series of subjects to be turned into postcards depicting the country and coast of the British Isles. It was a mammoth project. At first hè travelled in a horse drawn buggy but later resorted to exploring the countryside by bicycle. He produced nostalgic paintings in his own inimitable style; the scenes are romantic and picturesque, the colours are bright, even lurid, but every sketch is enlivened with finely drawn figures engaged in leisurely pursuits.

This venture brought him into Kent. He particularly relished the quaintness of Deal where he could fish from the pier and reminisce with the boatmen. Cards he produced numbered the 'Fountain Inn', once the haunt of smugglers, with its tangle of nets on the foreshore; the tumbledown cottage and smock mill at Upper Deal with a distant view of shipping in the Downs; a country cottage with a mother and her child at the garden gate watching a traveller with his dog pass the ancient church at Northbourne and seagulls wheeling over the wooden capstans and boathouses in the quiet fishing village of Kingsdown. Young is still remembered with affection by members of his large family. 'He was a huge chap', recalls his granddaughter, Barbara Boyd. 'Jovial and jolly'.

Perhaps the most desirable picture postcards from the Edwardian era were reproduced from originals by the artist, Alfred Robert Quinton (1853 - 1934). This prolific painter of British villages and landscapes worked almost exclusively for the publishing company, J. Salmon Ltd of Sevenoaks. He produced over two thousands paintings that were turned into popular postcards and he illustrated several topographical books. His colourful views of the seafront of Deal (reserved for the cover of this book) perfectly recreate the charm and beauty of a seaside resort in the halcyon days between two world wars.

Collecting picture postcards was probably the first of the indoor hobbies, ahead of coins, stamps, medallions and autographs to have universal appeal. They could be readily purchased from booksellers, stationers, newsagents, tobacconists, railway stations and hotel lobbies. Frequently, the only message scribbled on the card was: 'One for your collection'. Families gathered around the table to admire and discuss the latest acquisitions which were placed carefully into a leather-bound album. Publishers held competitions to encourage collectors, and winners of the greatest number of posted postcards far exceeded twenty thousand. Enthusiasm was fuelled by a magazine devoted to the hobby, 'The Picture Postcard', first published in 1900.

The craze ended abruptly with the advent of the First World War, with the lack of paper resources, rising production costs and restrictions on wartime censorship. When peace resumed, the increase in postage costs dealt a further blow. During the Second World War, albums were dumped for wastepaper salvage or destroyed by air raids. A revival of postcard collecting began in the 1970s when they were abundant and inexpensive to acquire. Collectors tend to concentrate on themes - film stars, railway locomotives, ocean liners, comic cards, trade advertisements or wartime propaganda - but it is the topographical views that inadvertently record for posterity that vanished world at the beginning of the 20th century. They present the halcyon days of Deal and Walmer which happily coincided with the period regarded as the 'Golden Age of the Picture Postcard'.

Post from

Deal and Walmer

The advent of flying in the early years of the 20th century allowed people to view Deal and Walmer from the air for the very first time. The accidental design of the Tudor rose at Deal Castle can be fully appreciated with the neat allotments of the Governor's Garden opposite. The long arm of the Victorian pier reaches out into the empty Downs Anchorage.

A later aerial view shows the Royal Hotel standing in isolation on Deal seafront. The single spire of St. Andrew's Church and the double spires of the Congregational Church (now the Landmark Centre) are dominant. Although this viewcard dates from the postwar period there are still plenty of fishing boats in evidence on the foreshore.

A view of The Beach at Walmer shows the grand seaside villas built when the railways opened up towards the end of the 19th century. On the right are the parade grounds of the Royal Marines South Barracks while on the extreme left is Green Park in the centre of Archery Square. It is the home of one of the oldest lawn tennis clubs in the world.

The garrison church of St. Michael appears alongside the playing fields in the centre of Royal Marines North Barracks while the chapel it replaced is shown just behind. In the distance St. Saviour's Church faces The Strand at Lower Walmer. Crossing the length of the bottom of the photograph is the railway line that linked Walmer to Deal in 1881.

ST. LEONARD'S CHURCH

A group of scouts pose before the high brick wall of St. Leonard's Church at a busy corner of Upper Deal. This Norman church was built circa 1080 and presents a confusing mixture of architectural styles: a 12th century nave, a 13th century chancel, a 17th century tower and a 19th century porch.

The red brick tower, surmounted by a white lantern with a cupola, appears on early charts of the Downs as an important landmark and for that reason it was maintained by Trinity House. Early maps show the tower with a steeple but this crashed through the roof in the 17th century causing immense damage.

UPPER DEAL

First Mayor of Deal was Joshua Coppin who lies buried in St. Leonard's churchyard. He lived at the adjacent Manor House whose interior boasted a magnificent carved oak staircase and a remarkable chamber 'fitted up like a cabin of a ship by a retired admiral'. From the rooftops, it was said, smugglers signalled secretly to ships arriving in the Downs.

Deal and Walmer once possessed seven windmills to supply bread and flour to ships in the Downs. Last mill to be constructed was at Upper Deal around 1855. It occupied an enviable position atop Mill Hill where it caught the wind in every direction. This slim, black, smock-mill, which had already been struck by lightning, was demolished in 1929.

Upper Deal

For centuries the main route from Upper Deal to Sandwich was along Middle Deal Road, North Sandy Lane (West Street) and the Ancient Highway. Many of the oldest properties are located there. 'Berkeley House', which is here viewed from the servants' quarters, was once owned by George Ludwig, Surveyor of Deal, who died in 1799.

London Road, Upper Deal.

There was an alternative, tortuous route via Sholden and Foulmead. Then it deviated along Finglesham and Ham before returning to Worth and finally Sandwich. In 1800, a direct turnpike road was laid from Upper Deal via Sholden, just west of Cottington, Foulmead and Worth to Sandwich. Houses soon sprang up along this busy main road.

SHOLDEN CHURCH

St. Nicholas' Church, Sholden, was built as a chapel-of-ease to St.Augustine's, Northbourne, although its actual date of construction is unknown. Over restored in Victorian times, this modest brick and flint church was devastated by a parachute landmine in 1941. A startling modern stained-glass window depicts this scene of devastation.

The interior is plain and light. There are numerous memorials to members of the ubiquitous Harvey naval family. One wall monument recalls Edward Banks, the Victorian cricketer, who lived at Sholden Lodge (now 'Hall') opposite. A talented gardener, he cultivated fuchsias and his 'Forget-me-not', is the emblem of the British Fuchsia Society.

DEAL CASTLE

Deal is the grandest of the three Tudor castles built 'to keep the Downs' from invasion after Henry VIII quarrelled with the Pope over his divorce of Catherine of Aragon. They were built in an incredible time - 18 months - and this included one of the earliest strikes on record when workmen downed tools and demanded a rise from 5d to 6d per day!

Built for the age of cannonfire, the castle retains its medieval features: a dry moat, a deep well, drawbridge, portcullis, iron-studded door and five murder holes through which boiling oil might be poured over the heads of invaders. Intended to repulse enemy warships, the first time the castle actually saw action was during the English Civil War.

DEAL CASTLE

Rows of semi-circular bastions, or 'lunettes', allowed a 360-degrees range of fire from the 'great gunnys'. The brass cannon's bore was 7 inches and its extreme range was almost three miles but shot from smaller guns, such as the falcon, travelled further but did less damage. At first, there was a delay in firing this armament for want of an 'Inginier'.

During the early 19th century an attempt was made to domesticate the fortress with the addition of a Governor's lodging on the seaward side. This entirely spoiled its medieval character and residents of the town were not entirely displeased when a German shell demolished it during the Second World War.

GOODWIN SANDS

The Goodwins are perilous sandbanks that lie four miles off Deal in the narrowest part of the English Channel. They are approximately twelve miles long and five miles broad. For most part they are concealed beneath the waves and present such a hazard to shipping that they have earned their fearful reputation as 'The Shippe-Swallower'.

At certain times of the year the Sands are exposed and it is then possible to walk across the hardened, rippled surface. Hardy boatmen have played cricket and football on the Goodwins but other sports include rugby, golf and bowls. Here a party of hairdressers are encountering a close shave on the quicksands.

Goodwin Sands

Over the centuries, the Goodwins have claimed hundreds of ships and thousands of sailors. A remarkable coincidence occurred when two ships - both named 'Mahratta' - were wrecked on the Sands less than one mile distant from each other. The first 'Mahratta' - wrecked in 1909 - was the largest ship ever claimed by the Sands.

S.S. 'Mahratta' was on the last lap of her voyage from Calcutta to Dundee with a diverse cargo when she went aground in Trinity Bay. Despite assistance from eight tugs and three lifeboats, she failed to refloat and inevitably split in two. Her sister ship, carrying a similar cargo and travelling an identical route, ran aground on Goodwin Sands in 1939.

LIGHTSHIPS

The Goodwins are considered so dangerous to shipping that Trinity House once marked them by four lightships: North Sand Head in 1795, South Sand Head in 1832 and East Goodwin in 1874. The Gull lightship indicated the fairway through the Gull Stream in 1809. Her name changed to 'Brake' when she was moored closer to Brake Sand in 1930.

A replacement Gull lightship was herself struck by a vessel in thick fog in March 1929 by the Ellerman liner, S.S. 'City of York', while making her way up Channel to the Pool of London. Captain Williams was drowned and the sleeping crew were cast into the icy waters but they were rescued by lifeboats. The stricken lightship was beached at Deal.

WRECKS

On 12 January 1911, the 60-ton Portuguese schooner, 'Flores', dragged her anchor in the midst of a storm. She hit the head of the iron pier where one of her booms carried away a gas lamp on the south-east corner. 'Flores' was then driven ashore at Walmer where she went quickly to pieces, scattering her cargo of chamber pots along the shore.

The period 'between the wars' was particularly eventful regarding local wrecks. It began with the wintry gale of November 1921 when the Finnish schooner, 'Kaleva', was blown ashore at the top of Exchange Street. At the auction of her remains held on the promenade the timbers and fittings sold for a mere fifty pounds to boatman Tommy Upton.

LIFEBOATS

First local lifeboat, 'Royal Thames Yacht Club', was placed at Walmer in 1856. Two later lifeboats were named 'Civil Service No. 4'. The first (shown here) was a self-righter built by Forrestt that came on station in 1885. She made a total of 56 launches before being replaced by another lifeboat of an identical name.

First lifeboat at North Deal was 'Van Kook', named after her donor, the marine artist, Edward William Cooke, in 1865. The lifeboat house with its lookout window and bell turret was not built until 1883. Today, it is the headquarters of the Deal Sea Angling Cub. The launch of North Deal's third lifeboat, 'Mary Somerville', attracted huge crowds in 1888.

LIFEBOATS

The lifeboat house on Walmer Green was built to shelter the third lifeboat, 'Centurion', that came on station in 1871. The second 'Civil Service No. 4' (shown here) was a self-righter built by Hanson of Cowes that saved a total of 155 lives before the station was temporarily closed in 1912.

In 1933, a revolutionary new motor-driven, beach launching lifeboat was introduced to Walmer. 'Charles Dibdin Civil Service No. 2' proved her mettle locally during the dangerous years of the Second World War. In the immediate postwar period with Coxn. Freddie Upton and Doctor James Hall aboard, she became the busiest lifeboat in Britain.

BOATMEN

These North End boatmen are scanning the horizon for wings of a wreck. They can be identified as (from left to right) Ned Hanger, Mon Hoile, Jack May (standing on the steps), Joe Marsh and Boss May (leaning against the boat). Far from being idle fellows, they bravely formed the crew of the lifeboat whose station appears in the background.

A group of 'Walmer Roaders' pose outside their boatshed adjacent to Walmer Green. These 'Sons of the Sea' are formed mainly from the redoubtable Pearson and Mercer families who regularly served as crew members of Walmer lifeboat. Several of them accompanied the second cross-Channel swim made by T. W. Burgess in 1911.

St. Andrew's Church

St. Andrew's was opened in 1850 to serve the maritime population of Deal. The subscription list was headed by the dowager Queen Adelaide, consort of William IV, who always held Deal in great affection. Built of Caen stone with a handsome tower and spire, the church was immediately recognised as a decided 'ornament to the town'.

The church endeavoured to offer spiritual comfort to local boatmen in their years of hardship and decline. There are several architectural features intended to complement these famous boatmen - the chancel arch is in the form of a clinker-built boat while the exterior stone lantern is shaped like a beacon to guide shipping safely into harbour.

CATCHES

SHAKING OUT THE SPRAT NETS.

Boatman tip out their vast catch of sprats from a drift net near the Royal Hotel. A thriving fish-preserving industry - converting sprats into sardines - flourished at the North End. Two rival firms - James Edgar and Wenceslas Chancerelle - employed 500 people and a fleet of luggers at the height of the spratting season: October to December.

Deal Boatmen.   4907 The "Wyndham" Series

An idle moment. Fishermen from the North End with a square prawn push net are leaning against a wooden capstan in front of the house called 'Seagirt'. The boatmen wear oilskins and sou'westers and one smokes a pipe upside down as a comforter. Long gone are the days of the heroic rescues by these celebrated 'Storm Warriors'.

CATCHES

Curious fish and mammals attracted by the warm coastal waters occasionally stray in from the Atlantic Ocean. Porpoises, dolphins and grampuses have been reported - lured by shoals of herring - gambolling in the Downs. Dicky Mercer holds the tail of a thresher shark - weighing 5 cwt and measuring 13 ft 9 ins - he caught on 22 September 1913.

Just as impressive as this thresher shark was the humpback whale sadly stranded at Pegwell Bay on 16 June 1922. Traditionally, these mammals are offered to the sovereign since they are deemed 'Fishes Royal'. When claimed, they are divided into three: the head for the king, the torso for the captor and the tail for the queen.

SEA BATHING

The invention of the bathing machine by Benjamin Beale, a Margate Quaker, in the mid-18th century focused the attention of sea-bathing on the south-east coast. The novel idea was that bathers could change in privacy in wooden huts which were wheeled down to the water's edge. Tommy Upton's bathing machines were a feature of Central Parade.

Beale's refinement - absent here - was the addition of a huge modesty hood that allowed shy bathers to swim in complete seclusion, shielded from public gaze. At Margate horses drew the cumbersome machines up and down the sandy beach but they were replaced by winches at Deal because the shingle shelves too steeply.

BEACH SCENES

This Edwardian lady is sitting watching her family shrimping near the ruins of Sandown Castle. At low tide large expanses of sand are revealed which gave rise to the name, 'Deal Sands'. In 1947, L.S. Lowry painted a composite scene northwards from the 'Royal Hotel'. The slim masts of beached boats echoed his trademark matchstick men.

Walmer beach has never been as popular with visitors and is used almost exclusively by residents. The boats are winched high up the shingle while the bathing huts stand at the water's edge. In the distance a steamer had called at Deal pier while the gazebo of 'Walmer Place, owned by Countess Stanhope, can just be glimpsed above the boats.

ENTERTAINMENT

White-faced clowns or 'pierrots', with their mixture of songs, dances and comedy acts, were a popular feature of Victorian and Edwardian summer seaside entertainment. They probably performed at the concert hall at the end of Deal pier although this jolly troupe appear to be posing formally in a photographer's studio with a country cottage backcloth.

The 'Astor Theatre' in Stanhope Road was previously known as both 'Stanhope Hall' and 'Winter Gardens'. It was later presented to the town as a war memorial by Colonel John Jacob Astor, M.P. This publicity photograph shows 'The Browns', a comedy musical company, performing on stage. The sender of the card wrote: 'Enjoyed them immensely'.

CINEMAS

Deal's first cinema, 'Marina Hall', was rivalled by 'Queen's Hall' in 1912. Astute manager, Arthur Sykes, changed his programme three times weekly to entice long queues into the domed entrance on Stanhope Road to watch favourite stars of the silver screen. In 1930 it became Deal's first talking picture palace and it was renamed 'The Plaza'.

The 'Regent', an iconic seafront building designed by Percy Levett, was opened to patrons in 1933. At that time it was Deal's largest cinema with a seating capacity of over 900. Most popular film was 'King Kong' starring Fay Wray which was shown repeatedly throughout the war to appreciative British and American servicemen stationed in the area.

St. George's Church is a handsome Queen Anne edifice that graces the High Street. Champion of its cause was Admiral Sir Cloudesley Shovel who was shipwrecked off the Scilly Isles in 1707. There are indications that it was intended as a 'Sailors' Church'. The east window depicts Walmer lifeboat in stained glass returning ashore after a rescue.

St. George's was intended as a 'chapel-of-ease' for St Leonard's Church at Upper Deal. When it was elevated to a parish church in 1852, its first Vicar was Rev. Henry Honywood D'Ombrain. An amateur rose grower, D'Ombrain founded the 'Rose Society'. Two of the roses he introduced are depicted on the inn sign of the 'Rose Hotel'.

This busy High Street scene shows a row of shops on the west side with their sunblinds shielding their crowded window displays from the scorching mid-morning sun. On the corner of Park Street is Giraud, stationer and stamp office, which also served as a subscription library. Giraud's had a second branch on the seafront opposite the pier.

Just past Deal Library is John Pittock, draper and outfitter. The premises, marked by a row of globe lanterns and rippling windows, occupies the site of Deal Playhouse. This was managed by the genial Sarah Baker and patronised by sailors stationed in the Downs. Ingloriously, the theatre ended its days as a second-hand furniture store.

Clarabut's was the main departmental store in the High Street. On Friday 11 October 1940, a busy shopping morning, four high explosive bombs were dropped there by the enemy, causing immense damage. One fell through the roof of Clarabut's but failed to explode. It was defused and displayed in the shop window for the remainder of the war.

High Street, once called 'Lower Street' because of its low-lying situation, appears as a lively shopping centre in this animated postcard. Clarabut's store appears on the left next to Northey's, stationer, which later jumped across the road to replace Hardy's. It is now Roper's which remains sandwiched between the 'Black Horse', and the 'New Inn'.

HIGH STREET

High Street, Deal

This view from above takes in the long line of the High Street towards the twin spires - 'Inspire', and 'Aspire' - of the Congregational Church (now the Landmark Centre). Opposite, and beyond, is the cupola above Huntley's, draper, bombed in World War Two. Horse and cart have given way to the motor car but tradesmen's bicycles are in evidence.

This substantial row of shops on the south side of Queen Street (formerly 'Five Bells Lane') was demolished for road widening owing to increased traffic between the wars. They include William's, saddle and harness maker, Romney's, baker and confectioner, and Inkerman's, beef and ham stores, later Laker's, bootmaker.

HIGH STREET

A view of the crossroads on the High Street before the installation of traffic lights. At the corner is the imposing dull brick National Westminster Bank. On the left is Darracott's, draper, with its florid painted signs and row of oval lamps advertising various wares, including carpets.

Having just pushed their pram over the crossroad, this trio of stylish ladies are heading towards South Street. Perhaps they have paused before entering the elegant Gaye's Cafe with its Italian coffee machine in the corner window? Its carved crescent moon and star is a most attractive feature of this once lamp-lined part of the High Street.

Another scene shows Lloyd's Bank at the corner of High Street and South Street. Next door is a Swiss confectioner's, with sunblinds obscuring its painted sign for 'creamed ice', and Long's, boot and shoemaker, beyond. Opposite is the vertical painted sign for Franklin's, draper, while trade handcarts wait outside Clifton's, family grocer.

South Street, a wide square at the southern end of the High Street, remains a bus depot although Carter House, the home of the author, Elizabeth Carter, has reverted from a hotel to a private dwelling. On the north side is Bourner's Garage, with its serried row of petrol pumps, and the art deco South Street Ice Cream Parlour.

Prospect Place, which became Victoria Road, once had a view or 'prospect' towards the Downs before Victoria Town Estate was built on the site of the former Navy Yard. A row of quaint dwellings still exclude a nautical air with their porthole windows and boat-shaped porches. The 'Deal Castle Inn', now a private house, was a haunt of seafarers.

Grand houses on the right of this once curving road formed the prestigious Victoria Town Estate. At the period of their construction, the tall villas were considered the height of fashion and the builders were immensely proud of their achievement. Florid features include portrait keystones, stained glass and ceramic tiles of exotic birds, fruit and flowers.

Baptist Chapels

First Baptist Church to be established in Deal was in Nelson Street. Later it became an organ factory. Victoria Baptist Church in Victoria Road - marked by the lady cyclist - was opened in 1881. The architect was John Wills of Derby. This most prosperous nonconformist church provided seats for 600 worshippers with galleries on all four sides.

Walmer Baptist Church on the Dover Road was opened in 1904. This occupied part of the 'Great Field' and worshippers had to cross orchards to attend services. Built in the Early English style in red brick with Bath stone dressing, its bold spire - 90 feet high - is a remarkable feature for a nonconformist church.

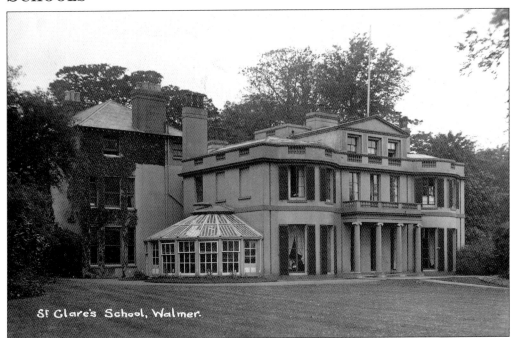

St. Clare's School, Walmer.

St. Clare standing proud upon the hill near to St. Mary's Church at Upper Walmer, was built by the Norwegian merchant, Andrew Gram, in 1806. At one time it was the enviable home of Lord Conyers. This beautiful mansion set in pleasant parkland became a successful preparatory school for boys under the direction of Alexander Murray in 1891.

Photo. Tourists Assn., Turnham Green, W.

St. Clare, Walmer.   (Large School Room.)

Murray's youngest daughter, Charlotte, poet and novelist, was one of the teachers. Among the pupils was Willie Mercer who became famous as the author, Dornford Yates. A later pupil was the comedian, Jimmy Edwards, who played the rascally headmaster in the television comedy, 'Whacko!'. The school eventually changed its name to 'Leelands'.

SCHOOLS

View of field with junior physical training class. Tormore. Upper Deal.

The grand private school opposite St. Leonard's Church at the foot of 'Rectory Road, Upper Deal, was called 'The Oaks'. Its was exclusively for girls and among the pupils was Dame Ninette de Valois, creator of Sadler's Wells (later 'Royal') Ballet. Later, it changed its name to 'Tormore' when it became a boys' school with extensive sports grounds.

Students from Deal College are preparing for a friendly cricket match on their field at North Deal under the watchful eye of the masters and a Royal Marine officer, presumably the sports teacher. The College, which gave its name to College Road, was situated at the bottom of Alfred Square. It is now a block of flats known as 'Lloyd Court'.

Roman Catholic Church

Adherents to Roman Catholicism, even after the Reformation, were always present in the port. St. Andrew's Hall in Duke Street was acquired for the occasional celebration of Mass in 1867. Later, land was purchased for a permanent church in Blenheim Road. The Church of St. Thomas of Canterbury was opened by the Bishop of Southwark in 1885.

The architecture is in the late Norman style. Features of the interior number a stone pulpit, a reredos with tabernacle over the Lady altar and a wrought-iron screen in the chancel with a niche displaying the statue of the Sacred Heart. In the 1920s, the colourful redecoration of the High altar in Renaissance style was hailed as the finest in England.

MINERS

After the discovery of coal during the borings for an experimental Channel Tunnel at Dover in 1890, four collieries were established in South East Kent. Betteshanger Colliery was the last pit to be opened in 1924. After the General Strike of 1926, militant miners walked from the North of England to the area seeking work and accommodation.

A vast housing estate - 950 semi-detached or terraced homes - were constructed atop Mill Hill for miners. Facilities provided included St. Richard's Church, Glyn Vivian Miners' Mission, Welfare Club and South Deal Primary School. Cycle and footpaths for the miners were laid along the Sandwich Road leading to Betteshanger Colliery.

GREAT MONGEHAM

Great Mongeham is viewed from the steps of the 'Leather Bottle'. On the left is a former dairy followed by three tiny cottages and another pub, 'The Friendly Port', now a private house. The 'Three Horseshoes', which once had a wrought-iron sign with three horseshoes, derives its name from the farrier, opposite, who would provide the fourth!

The farrier lived in this tumbledown thatched cottage which bears the date: 1735. This cosy dwelling has tarred cladding, shuttered windows, shy dormers and brick chimneys. In summer it is covered with clematis and honeysuckle. Next door, 'Sholden Bank House', retains its Kent peg wall tiles but its rich red bricks are now pebbledashed.

Baptists held services in the open air in the village until a permanent chapel was built. At one time worshippers rented a room in the converted malthouse for weekly services. The chapel, which dates from 1911, was constructed entirely by voluntary labour and most of the materials were donated so that when it opened it was declared free of debt!

'Pope's Hole' was once a quarry where chalk was excavated for building the Tudor castles. The present house that occupies the concealed site was built in 1939 by Lord Hore-Belisha, Minister of Transport, responsible for belisha beacons. Earlier, Mrs. Elliot, who owned these ramshackle cottages, ran popular tearooms in the deep, wooded hollow.

GREAT MONGEHAM

A wooden signpost at the fork in the road directs traffic to the villages of either Ripple or Northbourne. The pleasant paddock with its ancient mulberry adjoins the parish hall. Opposite is the 17th century 'Monk's Hall'. The curious name has never been satisfactorily explained although a painted figure of a monk once stood over the porch.

Mongeham Brewery and Dairy Farm is a splendid red brick Georgian property. It has a fanlight doorway, sash windows, dormer windows peeping through the slate roof and a date stone: 1735. The palings were replaced by a low stone wall since this area is liable to flooding. At the rear are the tall brick chimneys of 'Hill's Brewery'.

GREAT MONGEHAM

A view of The Street at Great Mongeham in the 1930s. The village stores-cum-post office displays a variety of enamel trade signs. Towards Ripple, the low thatched building was once a forge, the white painted thatched house dates from 1549 while, beyond, 'Lamp Cottage' was once the meeting place for the early Baptists. Opposite was a thriving farm.

The original Norman Church of St. Martin of Tours was rebuilt in the 13th century and again in 1851 by Butterfield. Treasures include the alabaster figure of William Crayford (died 1615) kneeling in armour; a helmet purporting to have been worn at the Battle of Hastings and a plaque with an inscription by poet laureate, Robert Bridges, to his nurse.

St. Augustine's, Northbourne, is one of the few cruciform churches in Kent. It was built in the 12th century on an earlier Saxon foundation. The Lady Chapel contains the monument to Sir Edwin Sandys and his wife (died 1629). Touchingly, the recumbent pair are portrayed holding hands. Curtains seal the church from draughts in winter.

St. Mary's, Betteshanger, is one of the most attractive Victorian churches in Kent. The architect, Anthony Salvin, effectively rebuilt an existing Norman church. Features that endure from the original construction include a 13th century piscina, the Royal Arms of William III and an early 18th century memorial with a naval theme to Salmon Morris.

COUNTRY CHURCHES

St. Nicholas', Ringwould, is perched high in a railed field with two ancient yews on the Dover Road where it commands a view of the sea. The 12th century church has a red tiled roof and a Kentish 'onion' dome on the tower which can be seen from far out in the Channel. Its flint tower was buttressed and ornamented with brick in the 17th century.

St. Mary's, Ripple, dates from the 13th century but it was extensively restored in 1861. In the churchyard lies Field Marshal, John French, First Lord Ypres, Commander of the British Expeditionary Force in 1914. He had been born at adjacent 'Vale House' in 1852. His sister, Charlotte Despard, suffragist and novelist, was also born there in 1844.

SOUTH EASTERN HOTEL, DEAL.

The 'South Eastern Hotel' (later 'The Queen's) was built by that railway company to accommodate travellers by steam locomotive to this seaside resort in 1886. Designed by James Brook, the sumptuous hotel boasted electric lighting, lifts to top floors and twin conservatories where silver service diners could enjoy enchanting views over the Downs.

THE
Royal Hotel,
DEAL.

Telephone No. 9

A bevy of maids pose on the verandah and a trio of waiters stand to attention while pampered guests lean on the steps or sit reading in the shade outside the historic 'Royal Hotel'. The postage stamp on the reverse of this trade card is dated '1908' and the telephone number of the hotel is given as 'Deal 9'.

'The Fountain' stood on the east side of Beach Street next to 'The Royal'. It presented a quaint appearance with its weather boards and staging overlooking the sea. A night bell was hung in a nearby alley to summon the Downs pilots who frequented the inn. 'The Fountain' acquired notoriety when the landlord was brutally murdered in 1905.

'The Crown' was another historic inn that extended across the full width of the North Parade. In prosperous times it was patronised by pilots whose headquarters were situated at the northern end. Inevitably it was demolished in the late 19th century to allow for road widening to accommodate increasing traffic at this narrow corner of Breach Street.

BEACH BOATS

Deal. North Beach.

Deal boatmen once relied upon a regular trade of servicing naval and merchant sailing ships sheltering in the Downs. The advent of steamships meant a decline in their industry and local boatmen turned to fishing and pleasure trips for employment. Here a boatman's family lean against their galley surrounded by rowing skiffs and galley punts.

1584. Central Parade and Beach, Deal

Locally-built craft numbered the sturdy luggers and cat boats and the swift galleys and galley punts. Before the arrival of the motor boats on Deal beach there was a rich variety of boats including foresail and mizzenmast galley punts, single-oared rowing skiffs and four-oared service galleys. All these boats were a distinctive feature of the North End.

Three children pose with their picnic baskets for the cameraman alongside the high wall of the Boatmen's Rooms. Opened in 1884, this was also the headquarters of the Deal and the Downs Branch of the Missions to Seamen whose chaplain was Rev. Thomas Treanor. A horse and cart is making a delivery to the adjacent 'Royal Exchange Hotel'.

'Seagirt' was an exposed gabled seaside cottage that stood at right angles to the shore. During the Second World War, it was fortified with a gun post since it came in the direct line of fire from enemy shipping. When it finally succumbed to the sea in the immediate postwar period it opened up the vista towards Sandown Castle.

Beach Street. *North Deal.*

All the windows are open on the high-rise rusticated terrace, with their balconettes, indicating that it is a fine summer morning. Respectable family folk stroll along the pavement contrasting strongly with the poorly dressed boatman shambling along the road. It is a clear indication of the changed fortunes of working-class folk at the North End.

THE BEACH, DEAL.

Galleys are drawn high up the shingle. Tall masts and flagpoles pierce the clear sky. Two men repair the transom stern of their sleek white galley punt. Again, the scene shows the decline of work among the boatmen of Deal. On the left are two inns - 'Lifeboat' and 'Forester' - but the third, 'North Star', is out of sight.

NORTH END

The beach at the North End is cluttered with boats, sheds, winches and nautical paraphernalia. The lifeboat house is a distinctive building with its oriel window and bell turret. It is hemmed in by a trio of pubs - the timber clad 'North Star', the since demolished 'Lifeboat' and the 'Forester', named after a lugger beached opposite.

A sailor pauses with his telescope before the Coastguard Station. The Coastguard, formed in 1821 to prevent smuggling, adopted a secondary life-saving role in 1856. The line of Coastguard cottages displays a primitive maritime art - bargeboards pierced with anchors and patterns in pebbles - to decorate their extended colourful seafront gardens.

Sandown Terrace (later 'Marine Terrace'), a substantial residential building with a sweeping bay and loggia, was constructed by William Betts, a railway contractor, in 1844. William Clark Russell, the great maritime author, lived here and wrote several novels with a local setting. 'You might fish with a rod out of the windows', he proudly declared.

Forty feet high waves lash the foreshore at the far North End knocking the lamp off its post! Crowds gather to watch the spectacle. On the right is the 'Sandown Castle Inn' since demolished for housing. The original public house, The Good Intent, that occupied this same site, served as the canteen for adjacent Sandown Castle.

SANDOWN CASTLE

2036 Deal   Ruins of Sandown Castle

Sandown Castle, one of the smaller Tudor fortifications, finally succumbed to the encroachment of the sea in mid-Victorian times, leaving only the towering walls of the landward bastion standing. It had been the prison of the regicide, Col. John Hutchinson, who signed the death warrant of Charles I. His ghost is said to haunt the crumbling ruins.

There was once a popular tearoom on the sloping lawn beside the ancient castle ruins Strollers along the northern extremity of the seafront were refreshed by cups of tea or ice creams while enjoying the breezy views - particularly the spectacular sunsets - across the Sandhills towards Sandwich Bay.

DEAL PIER

DEAL PIER.

There have been three piers to grace the foreshore at Deal. A great wrought and cast-iron pleasure pier was built to replace the timber jetty that stood north of the 'Royal Hotel' but succumbed to winter storms in 1857. The new pier was designed by the acclaimed architect, Eugenius Birch, whose credits include Brighton and Blackpool piers.

DEAL FROM PIER.

Local boatmen grumbled that the structure was a danger to shipping and hoped that it might be 'unscrewed'. Residents, however, appreciated the benefits it provided and visitors found it a welcome addition to the seaside resort. From the pierhead provisions were supplied to, and cargo landed from, vessels visiting the Downs.

DEAL PIER

The thousand foot long structure had seating along its entire stem, was illuminated at first by globe lanterns and incorporated a tramway for conveying luggage to waiting steamships. There were three decks - promenade, fishing and small boat - and at its seaward end was a cafe and a concert hall.

Everyone appreciated Deal's Victorian pier - lovers strolling arm-in-arm, explorers studying the coastline, invalids inhaling the bracing salt air. . . One visitor trilled: 'Here, on this pier, one can imagine oneself on the deck of some huge vessel in the Downs at anchor, enjoying the invigorating and life-giving effects of a sea voyage in the Channel'.

DEAL PIER

The annual Deal and Walmer Regattas have always been a highlight of the social calendar. They were instituted in 1826 by Captain Hugh Pigot in an attempt to ease the tension between boatmen and officers of the Coast Blockade (forerunner of the Coast Guard). Queen Victoria was an early patron of this novel aquatic event.

Luggers and galleys from along the South Coast competed in the rowing races while yachts entered the sailing contests from as far away as Cowes, Isle of Wight. One event eagerly anticipated was the Deal boatmen's race in which they participated in their famous eight-oared service galleys. Open to all, it was offered as a 'Challenge to the World!'

DEAL PIER

Sea angling, which originated at Ramsgate, soon spread along the coast to Deal which offered beach, boat and pier fishing. 'The Illustrated Sporting and Dramatic News' (10 December 1892) hailed it as: 'One of the best places for pier fishing on our south-east coast'. Here an angling competition is supervised by Mr. Lawrence, the Pier Master.

Fishermen on the lower deck of the pier brave the weather to pursue their favourite pastime. This photographic card bears Christmas and New Year greetings for 1909! Although all ages participate wrapped up against the elements in oilskins, the lady seems a little nervous of her husband's catch - a dogfish.

DEAL PIER

In 1940, the 350-ton Dutch motor vessel, 'Nora', carrying a cargo of straw boards, was struck by a drifting enemy mine and a vast hole was blown in her stern. Attempts were made to beach the crippled ship but a sudden storm swept 'Nora' northwards where she crashed broadside into the tremendous iron structure.

'Nora' remained a pathetic sight lying on her side, just north of the breached pier, for the rest of World War Two. Youngsters clambered aboard the stranded ship to slide down her upturned hull. The Royal Engineers, on Churchill's orders, demolished the remnants of the pier since they obstructed the field of fire from coastal guns after the fall of France.

DEAL PIER

4 DEAL. — The Pier. — LL.

The pier approach was always the centre of activity. Here folk take the early morning air along the promenade. A proud parent pushes her double perambulator after making sure her infants are shielded from the sunshine, a cloth-capped delivery boy pauses on his bicycle while children choose cherries to be weighed on brass scales from a trade handcart.

1811 Deal. The Esplanade.

A line of horse-drawn carriages with their padded seats and brass lanterns wait as a proprietor, wearing a suit with a watch chain in his waistcoat pocket, welcomes customers. A lad pauses with an iron hoop as a father with his daughter and her dainty parasol pass by. There is little to command the attention of the policeman on this fine summer's day.

This marvellous view of the seafront looking north from the pier shows 'Royal House', a baker's-cum-confectioner's owned by Richard Fox, which was inevitably demolished for road widening. Beyond the cluster of galleys, skiffs and punts are Tommy Upton's bathing machines which have negotiated the shingle and stand at the water's edge.

Lloyd's signalling station has been replaced by a ladies cloakroom which, in turn, will become the headquarters of the Angling Club. The sailing boat, 'Albion', is returning ashore crowded with sightseers who have enjoyed a brisk circuit of the Downs. Hotels invariably kept a pleasure boat for the enjoyment of their patrons.

2   DEAL. — From Pier. — LL.

This view from the pier looking south shows the long line of shingle and a sprinkling of locally-built boats - luggers, cats, galleys, punts - several with their sails set. The 'Port Arms' public house marks the beginning of the former Navy Yard that stretched along the foreshore towards Deal Castle.

1   DEAL. — View from Pier. — LL.

Leaning over the pier railings this view southward on a calm day takes in the line of the seafront with its plethora of shops, cafés and hotels. Most prominent is 'Beach House Temperance Hotel' on the far left. This was heavily fortified because of its position in the last war but demolished soon after to make way for a colourful municipal seaside garden.

PIER PARADE

Pier parade, with a strong easily breeze indicated by the flags flying horizontally, seems fairly quiet with a few residents walking along the promenade. A line of carriages awaits while their proprietor checks his pocket watch, hoping for customers. A shoeshine man stands idle, aided by crutches, although he, too, lacks customers.

Pier Parade now bustles with traffic. Horse-drawn charabancs are tightly packed with holidaymakers protected from the sun by canvas awnings while crowded motor buses rapidly transport residents along the seafront road. At one time a variety of conveyances might be hired including gigs, phaetons, wagonettes, chaises, flys and landaus.

The photographer has drawn back beyond the clipped hedges of the trim lawn beset with striped tents and marquees of 'Beach House Hotel'. Donkey Drew, to the right, a genial local character, is untethering his team ready to offer rides to adventurous visitors along the roadside.

Horse-drawn vehicles have almost entirely been superseded by motorised traffic in this later postcard dating from around 1920. In 1908, six motor buses - top speed 12 m.p.h. - were transferred from Birmingham to start regular services in Deal and district. The central roundabout was the terminus for coastal buses to Dover and Folkestone.

SUMMER HOLIDAYS

10 DEAL. — *The Parade.* — LL.

The flag on the tall mast at the pier approach proclaims it is blowing a strong easterly which is why the beach is deserted. Out for a stiff stroll, the trio of gentlemen, particularly the one in the centre with his three-piece suit, cane and bowler, commands attention. A woman in a white bonnet has turned quickly to face the camera, blurring the photograph.

1791 Deal.   The Esplanade.

A group of youthful folk seem happy to pause for the camera. They are a mixture of working-class residents and middle-class visitors. The pair of young men in their white duck trousers, striped blazers and straw boaters appear particularly dashing. The ladies in their long summer frocks, white gloves and veiled hats retain their elegance.

SUMMER HOLIDAYS

1796 Deal The Esplanade

All generations are represented in this crowded scene on the promenade. The mature lady with her floral hat and expansive bag is dressed entirely in bombazine and contrasts with the two young sisters with their white blouses and short pleated skirts. A pair of gallants in boaters, blazers and white trousers stroll purposefully towards the pier.

A crowded scene shows respectable folk enjoying a morning stroll in the sunshine. The elderly gentleman in the bath chair wears leather gloves and a bowler while the cloth-capped younger men carry gold chains in their waistcoat pockets. The ladies wear straw hats with artificial flowers, cherries, ribbons and veils.

BANDSTAND

A popular form of entertainment was the military bands that played in the bandstand on the seafront. Concerts most patronised were those performed by the Depot Band of the Royal Marines (who occupy the platform). Musicians wore small round caps with peaks edged with gold lace and scarlet tunics with gold lace edging and black trimmings.

Concerts took place in the ornate cast-iron bandstand set in a pretty railed garden immediately in front of the time-ball tower. This was swept away in 1928 when a pavilion was opened by Lord Beauchamp that allowed band concerts to take place in all weathers. For the moment, though, this respectable lady in her donkey cart can enjoy the music.

BANDSTAND

Vast crowds gathered. Notices were posted, roads were closed. The promenade was blocked with deckchairs for appreciative audiences. The ladies sat in their wide-brimmed straw bonnets with the parasols, fanning themselves with their programmes, while the gentlemen, sporting their monocles and moustaches, beat time with canes to the music.

This faded photograph gives a fascinating glimpse of the bandstand and its patrons who encompass all ages. Royal Marines not only take the stage but gather around as spectators. On the left is a sign for the gardens of 'Deal School' whose classrooms occupied the end block of Prince of Wales Terrace.

TIME-BALL TOWER

Deal's time-ball tower was originally built as the Royal Signalling Station around 1820. Atop the tower was a tall mast with two movable arms that might rapidly communicate coded semaphore messages, via a series of companion stations across Kent, until they reached the Admiralty in Whitehall. Alas, the line was never completed.

In 1855 the tower was equipped with a time ball that dropped at 1 p.m. daily via a signal transmitted from the Royal Observatory, Greenwich. This gave accurate time to ship's masters for them to set their chronometers needed to ascertain longitude on world voyages. Deal became the first place in the world to receive Greenwich Mean Time.

THE ESPLANADE

12   DEAL. — *The Parade and Beach.* — LL.

Folk stroll in their finery along the Esplanade in front of the Prince of Wales Terrace. Originally, this was the site of the Navy Yard developed over the centuries by the Admiralty to service their sailing ships stationed in the Downs Anchorage. It was swept away in the mid-19th century to make way for the prestigious Victoria Town Estate.

DEAL . PROMENADE & PIER

This lively photograph of the Esplanade was taken when motor cars had replaced horse-drawn carriages. The Italian ice cream barrow serves patrons of the bandstand. The high view shows the pierhead with its concert hall although the Downs is surprisingly empty apart from a handful of rowing boats and a stray Thames barge.

CROWDED BEACH

Crowds line the promenade and foreshore to cheer contestants at the annual Deal and Walmer Regatta. Traditionally, the events closed with a fireworks display and a grand ball, formerly held at the Assembly Rooms in Duke Street. South Coast regattas were discontinued at the start of the Great War but resumed almost immediately afterwards.

And even on an ordinary summer's day visitors flocked to the extensive beach along South Parade. The sails of a beach boat provide ample shelter for older folk while striped parasols shield young ladies from the searing sun as they doze in deckchairs. Offshore, boatmen row holidaymakers in their galleys along the coast on an unusually calm sea.

Beach Missions

Sea ports have always attracted religious societies, particularly Nonconformists. Beach missions were extremely popular in summer. Open air services contained a mixture of hymns, addresses, quizzes and competitions tailored to hold the attention of folk of all ages. Here, impeccably dressed and perfectly behaved children pose for the camera.

Adults in their Sunday best stand beside their deckchairs on the beach in front of Prince of Wales Terrace for another annual beach mission. The children - the girls in white frocks and bonnets, the boys in school uniform - sit obediently to pose once more beside their flag: 'Children's Special Service Mission' laid reverently on the shingle.

SOUTH BEACH

9   DEAL. — On the Beach. — LL.

Deal is in its heyday. It is the height of summer. South Beach is crowded with holidaymakers. Every age is represented from the elderly ladies dressed in black bombazine and bonnets to the young ladies in white cotton frocks with straw hats. The low building is the 'Port Arms', whose present inn sign depicts the town's coat-of-arms.

A double row of canvas deckchairs on the shingle are turned to face the promenade to watch folk pass by. . . There was a marked drop from the promenade to the beach and steps were placed at frequent intervals to allow access. The raised skirts and plunging necklines indicate that the photograph was taken one summer in the 1920s.

This photographic card was posted in 1938. These holidaymakers are therefore enjoying a last peaceful spell at the seaside before war broke out. Perhaps the splendid tripping boat is the 'Clarendon'. Harry Meakins, landlord of the 'Port Arms', is waiting for a full load before taking visitors for a trip to the Goodwins in his motor boat, 'Lady Beatty'.

Three fine tripping boats, including one just returned from an excursion, can be glimpsed in this extensive view of South Beach opposite the Prince of Wales Terrace. The one remaining tripping boat at Deal is 'Lady Irene' which was built for Harry Meakins in 1907. Now fully restored, it is regarded as the oldest beach boat in Britain.

The division between Deal and Walmer is midway through Deal Castle. Marine Road which follows the line of the seafront has a row of magnificent residences built when the railway lines reached this corner of the coast in Victorian times. 'Oakmead', which boasts a modern stained-glass window of a windmill, marks the site of Walmer Road Mill.

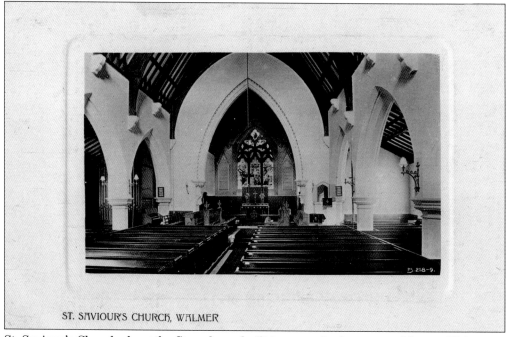

ST. SAVIOUR'S CHURCH, WALMER

St. Saviour's Church along the Strand was built to serve the boatmen of Lower Walmer in 1849. It was the inspiration of a fervent young curate, Rev. Henry Wilberforce, who was the youngest son of the anti-slavery campaigner, William Wilberforce. He readily persuaded the Duke of Wellington to be among the first subscribers to the new church.

WALMER STRAND

The Strand, Walmer

The Green is a pleasant open space adjacent to the sea which is greatly appreciated by the residents of Lower Walmer. A grand assortment of shops with their striped awnings - butcher, grocer, fishmonger, greengrocer, chemist, tobacconist, ironmonger, decorator - ensured that The Strand was a thriving community in the early 20th century.

THE STRAND, WALMER.

There were numerous inns - 'Lord Nelson', 'Lord Clyde', 'The Stag', 'True Briton' - and Reading Rooms to cater for Walmer boatmen. It was a tradition that, should the bell sound, shopkeepers opened their back doors so that members of the crew, who lived in the streets behind, could take a short cut to the lifeboat station on The Green.

WALMER. THE STRAND

Central was Loyns and Sons' Store, 'wholesalers and retail cash drapers'. It was divided into two departments: wines and spirits, costume and drapery. An advertisement in 'East Kent Mercury' expounded its wares: 'The latest novelties in French and English millinery, gloves and pongee silks for ball dresses, sashes and black silks for mourning'.

The Strand, Walmer.

The tip of St. Saviour's spire, containing a single bell, can just be discerned above the rooftops of the row of shops. During a thunderstorm in 1890, the church was struck by lightning that had destroyed this belfry. The boy whose duty it was to ring it prior to services had only just left his post. The shingled spire was later removed for safety.

WALMER STRAND

The Strand, Walmer.

A triangular green at the junction of The Strand, The Beach and Dover Road is now a municipal garden. After the First World War, a German field gun, captured at the Battle of the Somme, was placed there as a war trophy. This complemented the British Army Mark IV tank situated on the patch of land opposite the South Eastern Hotel.

ROYAL MARINE CHURCH PARADE, THE STRAND, WALMER   K 9501

This photograph was probably taken from the roof of Bank House at the far end of The Strand. The sweeping view takes in the line of shops, the lifeboat station and the Queen's Hotel adjacent to Deal Castle. The Royal Marines Band is leading a procession towards North Barracks in Dover Road to attend a church parade.

ROYAL MARINES

Royal Marines - 'soldiers that serve at sea' - were formed in the reign of Charles II by his brother, James, Duke of York and Albany (later James II) Lord High Admiral, in 1664. Detachments of Royal Marines were immediately stationed locally to defend the Navy Yard but their permanent base was established in redundant army barracks at Walmer in 1861.

Royal Marines Deal Depot consisted of North, South (or Cavalry) and East Barracks. North Barracks were distinguished by their immense colonnade while stables for horses remained in South Barracks. The two separate divisions - Royal Marines Light Infantry (RMLI) and Royal Marines Artillery (RMA) were not united as a fighting force until 1923.

ROYAL MARINES

East Barracks was formerly a Royal Navy Hospital. In 1809, during a thunderstorm, lightning was conveyed from the sails of Walmer Road Mill, to the topmost wards where it played around the patients' iron beds. Today it is an imposing building - 365 feet long - with rows of sash windows and a central portico surmounted by a cupola and clock.

An Infirmary was opened in Blenheim Road to replace the redundant Naval Hospital in 1900. It was built on the site of an old drill field where the Bicycle Corps formed by Major Edye in 1889 had practised their remarkable formations. Here a patient has been wheeled up to the decorated table to enjoy his Christmas lunch with the medical staff.

ROYAL MARINES

Royal Marines from Deal were engaged in the battles that accompanied the expansion of the British Empire. They participated in the Indian Mutiny, three Chinese Wars, Crimean War, Zulu War and Boer War. Their sworn aim was to protect the British Empire and since Britain was regarded as a Christian country regular church parades were obligatory.

Residents were proud of their association with the Royal Marines since their presence added prestige to Deal and Walmer. This culminated in the Honorary Freedom of Deal being conferred on them in 1945. A Royal Marine in full dress uniform appears as one of the supporters of the modern coat of arms for the Borough of Deal.

Royal Marines

Band of H. M. Royal Marines Deal.   J. Glencairn. Craik. Photo.

The Depot Band was formed in 1890 to join the Divisional Bands of Chatham, Plymouth and Portsmouth. Recruitment came from service bands, frequently the army, and civilian life. Its purpose was to provide music for ceremonial and social occasions, church parades and community events.

H. M. Royal Marines (DEAL) 1920.

A Victorian bandmaster marched with a range of instruments including french horn, trombone, euphonium, bombardons and drums. The Depot Band evolved into the Royal Naval School of Music. After the Second World War, this was restyled the Royal Marines School of Music whose later Directors were also Commanding Officers of the Depot.

The Church of St. Michael and All Angels in South Barracks was designed to hold one hundred worshippers. The foundation stone was laid by Lord George Hamilton, Captain of Deal Castle and former First Lord of the Admiralty. The Depot Church, which was identical in design to those at Eastney and Chatham, was consecrated in 1907.

Stained-glass windows, which featured warrior saints and armed angels, were designed by Kempe. The nave displayed colours of the Woolwich Division. Unfortunately, St. Michael's was severely damaged by a shell during an air raid in the First World War. Restored, it became the venue of regular concerts by the Royal Marines School of Music.

The Commander of the Royal Marines inhabited an imposing villa overlooking The Strand. Opposite was beached his personal galley. This was a long, sleek, white painted, six-oared craft built in Deal. The Commandant was also entitled to the services of a stylish horse-drawn carriage with an attendant groom.

The Royal Marines also owned a rifle range on the beach at Kingsdown. This had been in existence since 1859 when rent of one shilling was recorded but thirty years later a new lease was negotiated by the Admiralty. In 1903, the land was acquired by compulsory purchase and it was then employed for the temporary encampment of new recruits.

ROYAL MARINES

A highlight of the Deal Depot was when the Prince of Wales, as Colonel-in-Chief, inspected the Royal Marines on 4 May 1909. As King George V, he returned to inspect the newly formed 4th Battalion prior to their daring raid on Zeebrugge in March 1918. His Majesty directed that the Senior Squad should in future be designated the 'King's Squad'.

Empire Day, which fell conveniently on Queen Victoria's birthday (24 May), was yet a further excuse for a display of patriotism. Children of Royal Marines, who were taught at the Victorian Chapel School in North Barracks, were privileged to watch with their teachers the trooping of the colours by the Depot cadets on their playground in 1907.

ROYAL MARINES

Prior to the First World War, Deal Depot was put on high alert and buglers sounded the 'Assembly' in the streets of Deal and Walmer. The area was soon flooded with raw young recruits from across the country. A new unit, the Royal Naval Division, was formed and a Deal Battalion was created to replace the Royal Marines Artillery.

When peacetime resumed the training course for recruits could take a complete year. Royal Marines Light Infantry room mates (E10 'Birds') formed themselves into a band in their free time away from their nest. Improvised instruments include broom handles, frying pans, a trumpet and a penny whistle. Later inhabitants of E10 were known as 'Pigeons'!

A small army of cooks was required to feed the contingent of Royal Marines based at the three Walmer barracks. These seven cooks stand proudly in their aprons by the great vats for vegetables and roasting tins for joints in the cook house. They must be exhausted by the heat generated by such large ovens. The postcard dates from about 1910.

The Royal Marines always knew how to organise their own fun which they shared with the public. This was generally musically based. Here members of the band have dressed up in weird and wonderful costumes which seem to have a circus or pantomime theme. The comedy elephant has acquired the skill of playing a base drum with its trunk!

Royal Marines

Physical fitness was at the heart of recruitment and therefore trained instructors were paramount. In 1871, a Superintendent of Physical Training was appointed which led to the creation of the Physical Training School at Deal. The School was equipped with a sports field, drill shed, gymnasium and, later, a tidal salt water swimming pool along the Strand.

First Superintendent of P. T. was Captain J. Straghan RMLI who was trained by the Army. In addition to team sports, he was qualified to teach sabre, bayonet, boxing, vaulting and gymnastics. First Superintendant of Swimming was Lt. Farqueson RMLI who had saved the life of Midshipman (later Admiral) Jellicoe from drowning off Tripoli in 1893.

The Royal Marines at Deal rapidly acquired a strong sporting tradition. Their drill field in South Barracks was constantly employed for football, rugby, cricket, hockey, athletics, tennis, fencing and even horse riding. Competitive sports events, enjoyed alike by Royal Marines and civilians, always drew huge crowds.

The Royal Army Medical Corps are always represented wherever British soldiers are deployed in times of both war and peace. The Corps began to develop during the Boer War but reached a peak during the First World War. At Walmer, they arranged their own summer sports day when officers participated gamefully in a donkey race in 1908.

'The Globe Theatre' was built in a corner of North Barracks as an entertainment centre for the Royal Marines in the 1860s. This 'classic garrison theatre' was the venue for plays and concerts as well as gymnastic displays and boxing bouts. Charles Collins obtained permission to screen his animated pictures: 'As shown at the Marina Hall, Deal'.

The theatre was equipped with 400 seats for the troops and boxes at the rear of the gaslit auditorium for senior officers and their wives. Plays were performed by repertory companies and shows by famous stars prior to London's West End. Avidly awaited were the outrageous Christmas pantomimes performed by members of the Royal Marines.

36468. CHURCH PARADE OF THE ROYAL MARINES, DEAL.

The Royal Navy School of Music, which superseded the Depot Band, moved from Eastney into East Barracks in 1930. The school prospered and soon provided young musicians for forty ship's bands aboard cruisers, battleships and aircraft carriers. Bands were small and averaged twelve musicians because of the lack of space on board a ship.

Royal Marines march behind the band for a church parade just prior to the outbreak of hostilities. During the Second World War, Royal Marines manned two cross-Channel guns - 'Winnie' and 'Pooh' - on Dover Cliffs, St. Margaret's Bay and the coastal defence guns at Deal Castle. Also, 40 Commando trained at Deal before their epic raid on Dieppe in 1942.

ROYAL MARINES

Royal Marine Band, South Barracks, Deal.

Residents took pride in the presence of the Royal Marines in Deal and Walmer. Here the Depot Band has attracted a large crowd as it marches into Dover Road. The Union flag flutters in front of the Officers' Mess at South Barracks. Jubilee gate with its ornate lanterns and carved shields commemorates Queen Victoria's Diamond Jubilee.

Watched by a small band of spectators, the bandsmen lead the Royal Marines through Jubilee Gate for their Church Parade. They will turn to their left down Dover Road towards the seafront and then left again along Canada Road. Divine services were held at the Depot Church of St. Michael and All Angels in South Barracks.

'The Drum Inn', once stood atop Dover Road. Earliest mention of it was in 1720. A drummer boy drummed the troops back to Walmer Barracks during the Napoleonic Wars. This is a possible clue to the origin of its name. Although the ancient public house was demolished in the postwar period, this part of Walmer is still called 'Drum Hill'.

Reputedly, a tunnel used by smugglers for storing contraband ran from 'The Rattling Cat Inn' to Walmer Castle. The entrance was guarded by the landlord's cat that wore a string of bones around its neck. If the Revenue Men broke into the tunnel, the cat would spring along the passage, the rattling of the bones warning the smugglers to escape.

DOVER ROAD

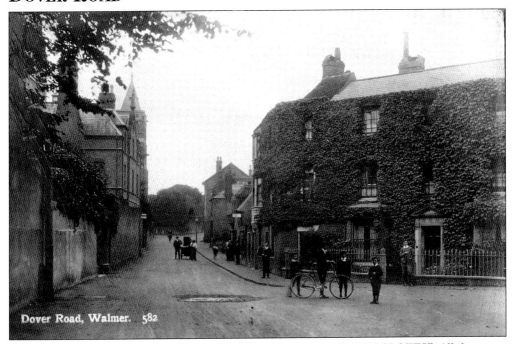

Dover Road at the junction of Church Street bears the signs: 'DRIVE SLOWLY'. All the same there is little traffic in evidence. The decorated tower of the Roman Catholic Church erected in 1881 remains although the convent buildings were demolished for road widening. At an angle are the grand 'Church House' and the slender 'Tollgate Cottage'.

The narrow lane atop Dover Road is hardly recognisable from today's main road. A handcart is parked in front of a row of shops and a donkey emerges from round the corner. Pickard's, family butcher, owned the premises with the wrought-iron canopy while next door was Woodcock's, general stores, displaying an abundance of enamel trade signs.

Old St. Mary's

Old Church, Walmer

Old St. Mary's in the village of Upper Walmer is a Norman gem. It was built (circa 1120) by the d'Auberville family, the ruins of whose moated manor house is visible from the churchyard. Originally the church consisted of a nave and chancel with north and south doorways. A lofty Norman doorway is concealed by a later porch.

8   WALMER. — Old Church. — LL.

The Duke of Wellington, when resident at Walmer Castle, was a regular worshipper. He rode over from the castle, a great Bible tucked under his arm, and tied his horse to an ancient yew near the porch. Then he would curl up in a corner of his private pew under the pulpit (since demolished) and fall asleep during the long sermon, snoring loudly.

New St. Mary's

An increase in the congregation in late Victorian times resulted in the building of a larger church atop Constitution Hill. New St. Mary's was built of Kentish ragstone with Bath stone dressing from designs by Sir Arthur Butterfield. The grand bell tower was intended as a memorial to Earl Granville, Lord Warden of the Cinque Ports.

Walmer.   Interior of St. Mary's Church.

Built in the Early English style, the impressive interior consists of a wide, lofty nave with arcades of five arches opening onto two side aisles, a chancel and a baptistry. There is a local Browne's organ, choir stalls of rare sequoia wood and spectacular stained-glass windows. The church, which seats 600 parishioners, 'smacks of Victorian triumphalism'.

WALMER GREEN

A sturdy wooden capstan dominates this scene of the seaward side of Walmer Green. The lifeboat station is garlanded for a special occasion but there is no sign of the lifeboat. There is an assortment of fishing boats and clutter of boatmen's paraphernalia. A Coastguard with a telescope under his arm pauses to chat with a young gentleman.

Coastguard Station, Walmer

The Coastguard Station that consists of a collection of weatherboarded huts is marked by a flagstaff that flies the white ensign at its peak. A long brick building on The Green housed the 'Board of Trade Rocket Life Saving Apparatus'. In the distance, opposite the lifeboat station, appears St. Saviour's Church, still sporting its shingled spire.

WALMER GREEN

The lifeboat station has always been a meeting place for strollers on sunny days. Again, there is no sign of the actual lifeboat. A group of Walmer Roaders are leaning idly against their wooden capstan while their luggers and galleys are beached high upon the shingle. In the distance landing stages of the pier have been revealed by the low tide.

A Coastguard, boatmen and their dog examine the upturned hull of a galley on Walmer beach. There is little sign of activity. Behind is the pleasant row of dwellings that line The Beach. In the far distance is the turret of Walmer Place, former home of the Countess of Stanhope, who was a close acquaintance of the Duke of Wellington.

THE BEACH

The Beach at Walmer presents a long line of attractive Victorian and Edwardian residences many of which have their own secluded seafront gardens with summer houses. The path on the seaward side that runs from Deal to Kingsdown marks a track formed by the Coastguard in their determined attempts to patrol the lonely beach against smugglers.

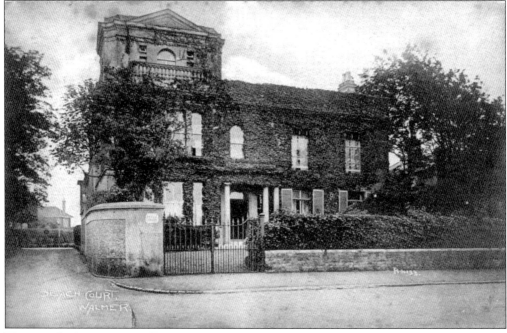

The grander houses along The Beach, which ends with the magnificent Beach Court, were mainly constructed when the railway opened at Walmer in 1881. John Hassall, pioneer of poster art, was born in one of these splendid residences in 1868 while Lord Lister, pioneer of antiseptic surgery, died at No. 32, 'The Coast House', in 1912.

LOWER WALMER

Liverpool Road, Walmer. 1986.

A horse-drawn delivery cart winds its way along Liverpool Road behind Walmer Castle. A pleasant meadow with its belt of trees faces the entrance to 'Liverpool House', a private residence once owned by George Leith who leased it to successive Lords Warden, including Lord Liverpool, to supplement the scant accommodation for guests at the castle.

Walmer.   St. Mary's Church.

St. Mary's Church crowns the hill across the wide expanse of The Glen. The centre path leads upwards towards a renowned beauty spot, Hawkshill Freedown, where troops from Walmer Castle were drilled by their commander, Captain Hawke, in the 16th century. Because of its approximation to France, this became an airfield in the First World War.

WALMER CASTLE

Walmer Castle is a smaller fortress than Deal. It has only four semi-circular bastions (or 'lunettes') arranged around a circular keep. It is thought that the design of these Henrican Castles was based upon the emblem of the Tudor rose. This pattern can be observed from the air along with the kitchen gardens, dry moat and governor's lodging.

Walmer Castle was domesticated when it became the official residence of the Lords Warden of the Cinque Ports. First resident Warden was Lionel Sackville of Knole who succeeded Queen Anne's dull consort, Prince George, in 1708. Famous Wardens number William Pitt, Sir Winston Churchill and Queen Elizabeth, the Queen Mother.

WALMER CASTLE

WALMER CASTLE, FROM THE LAWN.

A particular pleasure of Walmer Castle is the extensive grounds originally laid out by that eccentric niece of Pitt, Lady Hester Stanhope. 'I am not dull or, rather, not idle', she once declared. 'I have the charge of improvements here - plantations, farms, buildings.' She converted the stone quarry beyond the paddock into a scene of 'great rustic beauty'.

Broad Walk, Walmer Castle.

Hester's fine achievement was continued by Lord Granville. During his wardenship in the 1860s, he added the tree-lined drive and adornments to the gatehouse that rendered a softer tone to the formidable fortress. Particular pleasures of Walmer Castle are the undulating yews and the herbaceous borders of the Broad Walk.

WALMER CASTLE

Walmer Castle.   Duke of Wellington's Room.

Arthur Wellesley, First Duke of Wellington, was Lord Warden for almost one quarter of a century (1829 - 1852). The Duke took immense pride in this prestigious appointment and spent every autumn in his 'charming marine residence'. He surprisingly endeared himself to residents who greatly grieved when he died at the castle in 1852.

WALMER CASTLE.
THE DUKE OF WELLINGTON DIED IN THIS ROOM. THE
BOOTS ARE THOSE WORN AT THE BATTLE OF WATERLOO.

A later Lord Warden, W.H. Smith, First Lord of the Treasury and Leader of the House of Commons (but more famous as founder of the stationery firm) collected relics of the Duke's occupancy. These included the desk at which he stood to write, the camp bed that accompanied him on campaigns and the winged armchair in which he died.

WALMER CASTLE

WALMER CASTLE NELSON RECEIVED HERE HIS INSTRUCTIONS FOR THE BATTLE OF TRAFALGAR.

Part of the sitting room overlooking the Downs has often been referred to as 'Nelson's Corner' and furnished with supposed artefacts of the Vice Admiral. Although Nelson certainly called at the castle early one morning when he was preparing his French Campaign in 1801, he was not admitted since Prime Minister 'Billy' Pitt was fast asleep!

Queen Victoria and Prince Albert and their first two children spent a late summer holiday at Walmer Castle in 1842. The young royal couple - deeply in love - enjoyed carriage rides around the countryside and invigorating walks along the seafront away from the gaze of inquisitive crowds along the foreshore towards Kingsdown.

KINGSDOWN

The fishing village of Kingsdown-on-Sea snuggles under the shelter of the celebrated White Cliffs. The first lifeboat, 'Sabrina', came on station here in 1866. She was the smallest craft ever built by the RNLI. Her cox'n was Jarvist Arnold who, in 23 years of service, saved over 100 lives from the sea. The lifeboat house is now a holiday home.

The village had a reputation for smuggling and wrecking which allegedly took place in that northern part of the village immediately under the cliffs known as 'Old Stairs Bay'. Wisely the Admiralty decided to protect this remote coastline by establishing a Coastguard Station complete with watch room, boathouse and ten cottages for dedicated officers.

KINGSDOWN

North Road is lined with quaint boatmen's cottages that incorporate sail lofts, herring hangs and net drying sheds. Two roads - North and South - are linked with narrow paths - Shrimp Lane and Pig Sty Alley. The village once boasted four public houses but 'The Victory' closed its doors to customers after the Second World War.

'The Zetland Arms' was named after either Lawrence Dundas, First Earl of Zetland (1766 - 1839) or his son, Thomas, Second Earl (1795 - 1893). Unusually, this public house sits on the beach and is liable to flooding. One-time landlord was Jarvist Arnold, cox'n of the Kingsdown lifeboat, but here a later landlord, William Wellard, poses with customers.

KINGSDOWN

South Road with its single row of former boatmen's cottages reached by a shingle cart track bears the brunt of winter storms. At the seaward corner is 'Kingsdown End'. This was once a general store-cum-post office run by Duncan Pittock. He was licensed to offer for hire a fleet of landaus and victorias and also advertised 'Good stabling'.

At the turn of the century there is still evidence of a strong boatmen's community with their huts and boats beached on the shingle. The villagers seem content to spill out onto the road for the photographer. A paddle steamer has just left Deal Pier to take passengers on a coastal trip around the South Foreland.

KINGSDOWN

A picturesque corner of the village is The Rise, once called simply Kingsdown Lane. The house with the open window also changed its name from 'Hillside' to 'Blackacre'. A shared well is located in its garden while the neighbouring house, 'Climbdown', has a pump in its yard. Schoolgirls have wandered down the hill from St. Monica's School.

Upper Street with its charming row of 18th century farm cottages has hardly changed in almost a century. Reputedly, 'Robin Hill' and 'Rose Cottage' had links with smuggling. Certainly, the bucket of the well at adjacent 'Well Cottage' once surrendered a hidden cache of French kid gloves. A third public house, 'King's Head', stands on the right.

KINGSDOWN

Perched on the clifftop is the Victorian Church of St. John the Evangelist. It was built in high Gothic style by William Curling, a wealthy shipowner who lived in Kingsdown. The interior is plain and simple with neither aisles nor chapels but it is remarkably light and colourful. Numerous stained-glass windows commemorate members of the Curling family.

William Curling resided at Kingsdown House at the foot of the hill leading to the village. He was a great benefactor and presented the rectory and the schoolroom. When he died in 1853, his widow continued to teach there but the building is now the village hall. His grand villa set in extensive grounds became a holiday camp in the postwar period.

KINGSDOWN

Kingsdown Cliffs with its views over the English Channel towards the French coast proved an ideal place for camping. This postcard, signed on the reverse by members of the 12th scouting group at Kingsdown, was posted in July 1960. The message reads: 'Weather good but windy. Rained heavy last night. Bathing beach below site'.

'The Rising Sun' is still an enticing weatherboarded hostelry although it is no longer served by the Walmer Brewery, Thompson and Sons, whose motif was the South Foreland lighthouse. At one time a carved sunburst replaced this desultory signboard. A vehicle of the British Motor Company awaits to return passengers via Walmer Castle to Deal.

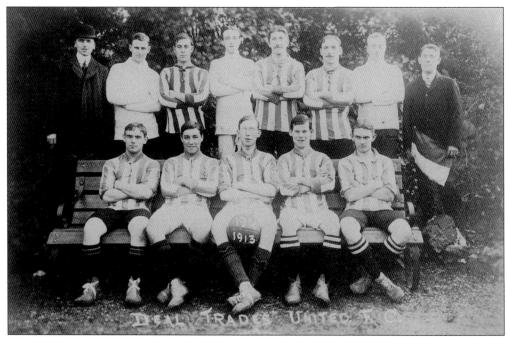

Deal Town Football Club started as Deal Cinque Ports Football Club in 1908. It plays at the Charles Football Club presented by the town's great benefactor Sir Ernest Justice Charles. Almost every section of the community - schools, churches, boatmen and tradesmen - at one time formed themselves into a football team.

'Deal and Walmer Angling Association', which is one of the oldest in the country, was begun in 1905. Enlisted men, recognising they could not compete with their superior officers, formed 'Deal Angling Club' soon after the First World War. Mackerel, dogfish, whiting, plaice and cod are among the prized and plentiful catches in the Downs.

The gentle pursuit of bowls is greatly enjoyed by older residents. There are three local bowling clubs: Deal Bowling Club (1924), Victoria Park Bowling Club (1948), and Betteshanger Bowling Club (1933) that occupies a corner of the Welfare Sports Field atop Mill Hill. Deal Bowling Club was in Victoria Park until it moved opposite to Mill Road.

In 1892 the Cinque Ports Golf Course was formed on land in the sandhills north of Sandown Castle. The Prince of Wales (later George V) played a round or two on the links when visiting Deal in 1909. The occasion was marked by adding the prefix 'Royal'. Another Prince of Wales (briefly Edward VIII) also regularly patronised local golf clubs.

GROUPS

Healthy and hearty scouts pose before their tents on Freedown at Walmer. First troops started in Deal around 1908 but because various scouts here sport the war service badge this photograph must date from after 1919. The group includes a pair of rovers dressed in kilts with sporrans, an army officer and an elderly lady who is guest of honour.

The 6th Deal Company of Girl Guides, which was formed in 1927, proudly pose with a challenge cup won for either a swimming or rally competition that might involve signalling, drill or first aid. The Guide Captain, Miss Daisy Mary Homeward, and her Lieutenant, Miss Winifred Jane Reece, are sitting behind the trophy. The company was disbanded in 1931.

GROUPS

Deal Borough Police Force, which was established in 1857, was merged with Kent County Constabulary in 1889. In this official photograph the officer in the centre is the Superintendent while the officer standing on the right with his drawn sword is from the Mounted Branch. Officers wearing forage caps are from Kent Cycle Unit formed in 1896.

Deal's Post Office was situated in Park Street before it moved to the stately red brick building with the distinctive crow-stepped gable in Stanhope Road in 1909. These postmen, several of whom sport long service stripes, will have delivered cards in this collection. Younger postmen have formed themselves into a football team.

The stretch of seafront north of the 'Royal Hotel' was reserved for residents. Prior to World War Two, it was still a lively community with an assortment of public houses, hotels, shops and houses: 'Woodstock' (marked), 'Trafalgar House' (home to the wartime humorist Nathaniel Gubbins), Nelson's Cottage', 'My Lady's Cottage' and 'St. Elmo's'.

An enticing row of seafront businesses includes Oatridge's, pastrycook, and Outwin's, newsagent, that attracted customers along Pier Parade. Both were bombed during the Second World War and were replaced by 'The Quarterdeck'. An advertisement for East Kent Motors indicates that the pier head was the starting point for No. 1 Town Service bus.

'The Queen's Hotel' survived war time hostilities and continued to attract affluent patrons for several decades. The splendour of the cast-iron porch can be appreciated in this postwar postcard. Poet Laureate, Sir John Betjeman, influenced its status as a listed building but, sadly, arsonists destroyed it. The site is now a block of luxury flats.

This sweeping view shows the popular promenade in the immediate postwar period. The pair of forlorn toll booths remains as a memorial to the Victorian pier. An Austin Cambridge makes a precarious circuit of the roundabout heeding the plethora of 'Keep Left' signs but no longer requiring the wartime painted markings on the triangular island.

BIOGRAPHY

GREGORY HOLYOAKE is an actor, author and teacher who lives on the seafront at Deal. He studied as a schoolmaster at Culham College of Education, Oxfordshire, where he gained teaching diplomas in English Literature and Divinity. As an actor he trained at Rose Bruford College of Speech and Drama, Kent, before embarking on a theatrical career, appearing in tours and repertory nationwide.

Gregory has been a photojournalist for forty years and he has appeared regularly in national magazines including 'Country Life', 'Country Homes and Interiors', 'Illustrated London News', 'This England', 'The Lady', 'Heritage', and 'Evening Standard'. He began by writing the children's pages of 'The Observer Magazine', sharing the end pages with Peanuts!

For five years Gregory was chief reporter for 'Kent Life' where he became an authority on Kentish subjects. He photographed 'Kent ~ The County in Colour' for Dovecote Press and 'Scarecrows' for Unicorn Press. He has also written the history of Deal in two volumes - 'Sad Smuggling Town' and 'All in the Downs', published by S.B. Publications.

Gregory's postwar childhood is told in 'The Prefab Kid', also published by S.B. Publications. This has been printed several times including a large print edition for libraries. The author was born in 'Redan', formerly 'The Clifton Temperance Hotel', the gardens of which are shown in this faded photograph below.

The tea gardens of 'Redan' Temperance Hotel.